ARIEL GUZIK

Holoturian

ARTS CATALYST

Edited by Nicola Triscott

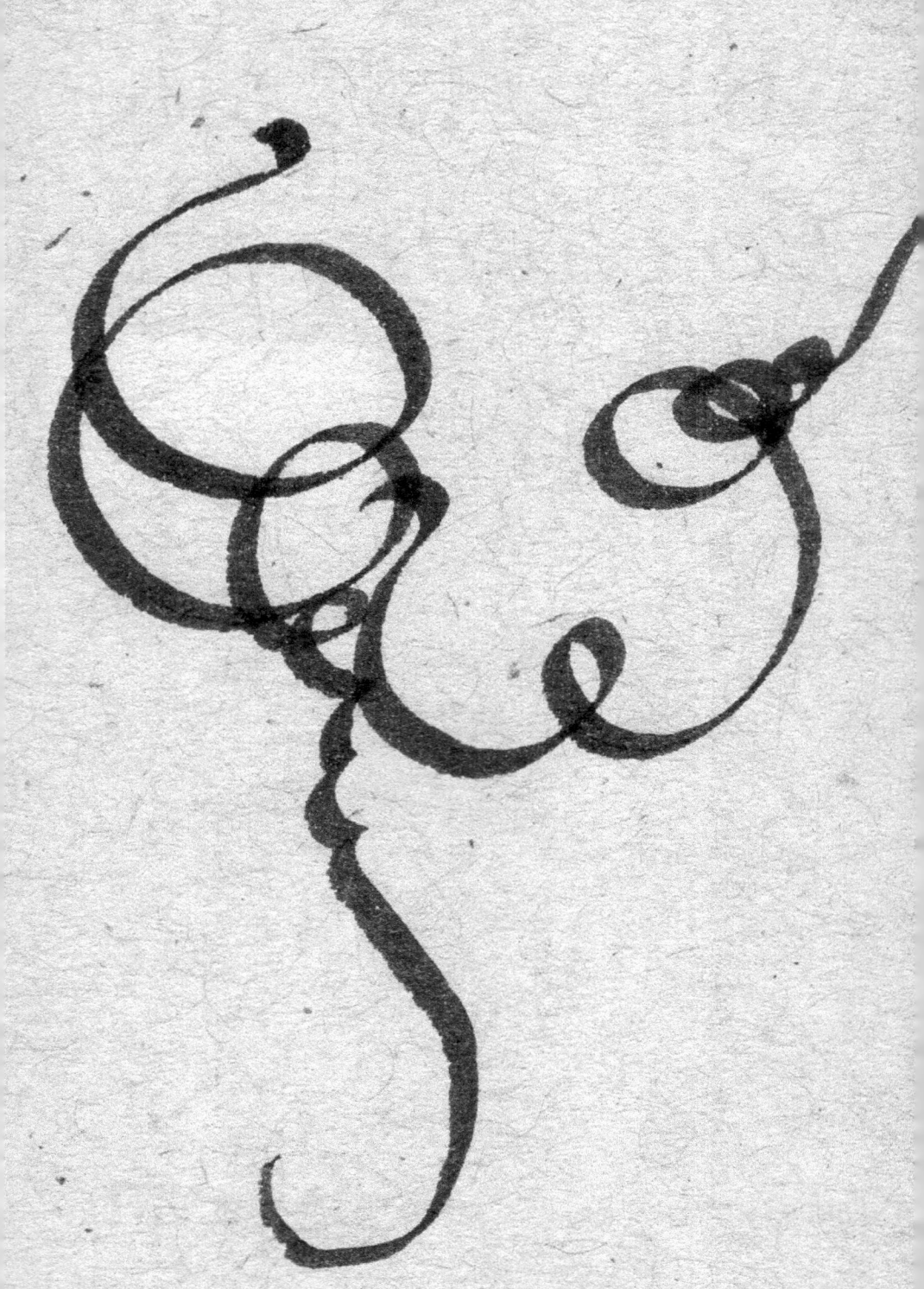

The Re-enchantment of the Ocean: Ariel Guzik's Cetacean Encounters by Nicola Triscott

p.9

Seas of Sound by Mark Peter Simmonds

p.25

Plates

p.33

This publication follows the exhibition 'Ariel Guzik Holoturian' at Edinburgh Art Festival 2015, commissioned by Arts Catalyst and Edinburgh Art Festival.

Contributors:
Ariel Guzik (member of FONCA'S 2012-2015 Sistema Nacional de Creadores y Artistas)
Nicola Triscott
Mark Simmonds

Editor
Nicola Triscott

Design
Margherita Huntley

Proofreading
Patricia Hallam

Published by
Arts Catalyst,
74—76 Cromer Street

www.artscatalyst.org

ISBN 978-0-9927776-8-5

Nature's Expression and Resonance Research Laboratory. Ariel Guzik, Catalina Juárez, Emilio Gálvez y Fuentes, Alejandro Colinas, Leobardo Ramírez, Adriaán Schalkwijk, Luis Alonso, Teresa Carter, Carmen Pineda, Alberto Navarro, Raúl González, Marcela Armas, Gabriel Acosta, Esther Heras, Dalia Huerta, Beatriz Beltrán, Aurora Rubio.

Thanks to
Gillean Dickie, Mark Peter Simmonds OBE, Sorcha Carey, Jon Clarke, Professor Paul Thompson, Jimena Lara Estrada, Gabriela Garciadiego, Rob La Frenais, Jareh Das, Claudia Lastra, Jessica Wallis, Alec Steadman, Gary Sangster Susan Chapman and Rocio Bermejo (Anglo Mexican Foundation).

FRONT COVER *Holoturian* Exhibition, Trinity Apse. Edinburgh Art Festival, Adriaán Schalwijk, 2015

ENDPAPER *Women of the sea (Mermaid)*, Ariel Guzik, 2015

The Re-enchantment of the Ocean: Ariel Guzik's Cetacean Encounters
by Nicola Triscott

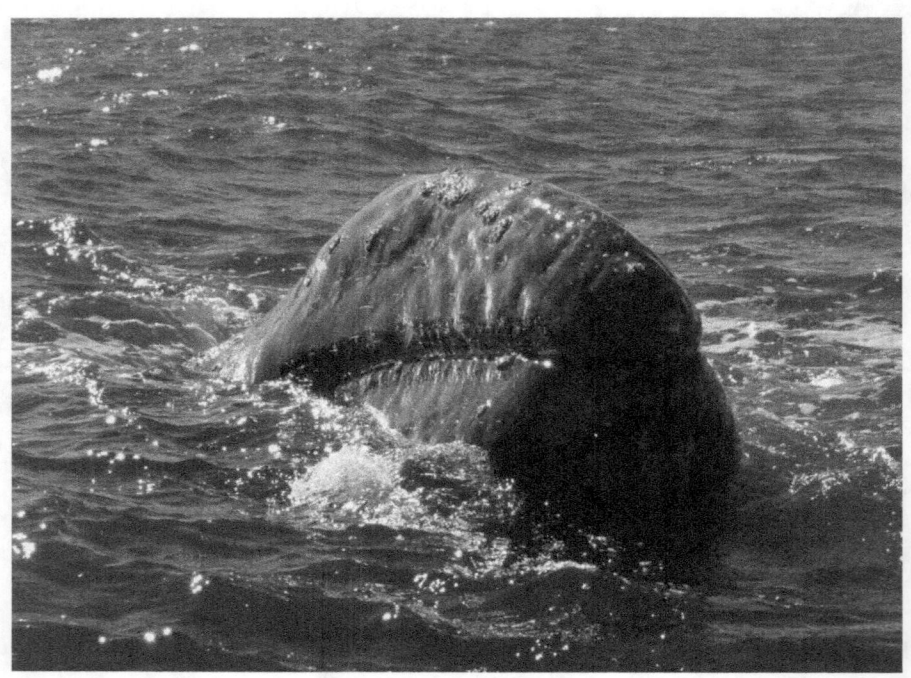

Ballena Gris, Baja California Sur,
México. Photo: Raúl González, 2002

"... meetings make us who and what we are in the avid contact zones that are the world." Donna Haraway

For more than ten years, Ariel Guzik, a self-taught artist, inventor, musician and researcher, has been seeking a way to communicate with cetaceans — dolphins and deep ocean whales — in the wild. He considers this research a natural progression from his long-term inquiry into the languages and resonances of nature, which has taken the form of designing exquisite and sophisticated instruments that are able to convert signals from the natural world, including the electrochemical impulses of plants, the movements of clouds and the sun's rays into subtle sounds and harmonious vibrations.

Through his delicate sound installations and performances, Guzik invites people to sense the physical, emotional and spiritual relations between plants, animals, nature and humans. As a musician, he creates gentle, melodic, haunting sounds. As a researcher, his interest lies in exploring the phenomena of resonance, electricity and magnetism as foundations for the invention of mechanisms that can connect us to nature through music.

Guzik was drawn to whales and dolphins because of their status in the contemporary imaginary as beings of spiritual force, memory and wisdom. Through history, whales and dolphins have played a large role in the culture of residents near sea areas and islands, the smaller species in particular entering into the mythology of these people because they could be seen from the shore or encountered from small boats. In Greek mythology, dolphins are reported rescuing many people from drowning. They were also said to have a particular love of music, probably because of their own song, and legends tell of dolphins saving famous musicians such as Arion of Lesbos. The great whales were known in ancient times primarily from whale strandings or descriptions by mariners. Whaling tales from the 17th to 19th century tend to describe battles between sailors and harpooned animals, self-servingly representing whales as fierce sea creatures. Literature of the time, including the novels *Moby Dick* by Herman Melville and *20,000 Leagues Under the Sea* by Jules Verne, also represent whales as monsters from the deep. But during the 20th century, with more research, whales became understood as intelligent and peaceful creatures. Dolphins too were increasingly represented as symbols of animal intelligence.

8   In 2007, Guzik completed the construction of a prototype underwater musical instrument designed to interact with cetaceans, which he named *Nereida*. *Nereida* is a fused quartz capsule with a core mechanism of cords and circuits. It is lowered into the sea from a drifting boat with the intention of establishing contact and forming a kind of gentle link with cetaceans through music. The artist tested Nereida several times in the Sea of Cortez (Gulf of California), each time experimenting with the capsule's sonic capabilities and observing the cetaceans in the locality — mostly bottlenose dolphins and gray whales. In later expeditions, Guzik's team began using hydrophones to listen to and capture the sounds made by these animals. He points out that, while these recordings may be of interest to scientists, it is not his purpose to make a scientific study but rather to establish a non-invasive encounter with these ocean creatures.

Ariel Guzik's studio is set a beautiful old house in Mexico City. Its rooms hold a phantasmagoria of the artist's intriguing resonance instruments, an electronics workshop and a herbarium, set around a courtyard garden. Here, the artist tells me about his most extraordinary encounter with cetaceans, which took place off the coast of Costa Rica in 2014 onboard the Aguila research yacht, captained by Nico Ghersinich. On one remarkable night, the drifting boat with its submerged *Nereida* capsule became surrounded by a very large number of dolphins and whales that coasted with them for many hours. At first Guzik did not have a hydrophone to record the sounds taking place below the ocean surface but, realising the unique nature of this encounter, the crew made radio contact with some oceanographers and were able to locate a buoy used for scientific research and borrow their hydrophone.

The recording made that night, which the artist played to me, is astounding. It is apparent, even to the uninitiated ear, that there is a large number of cetaceans in the vicinity. Over the subtle chiming tones of *Nereida*, a 'choir' of dolphins' whistles of frequency-modulated pure tones is heard, underlain with the deep reverberations of humpback whales, probably present at a far greater depth. The serendipitous intermixing of tones and sounds gives the impression of a musical performance, as though this sound-based community is harmonising with *Nereida*'s chimes.

Since my first meeting with Guzik and my experience of an installation containing his *Nereida* capsule at a festival in Mexico City, I was captivated by the possibilities and meanings

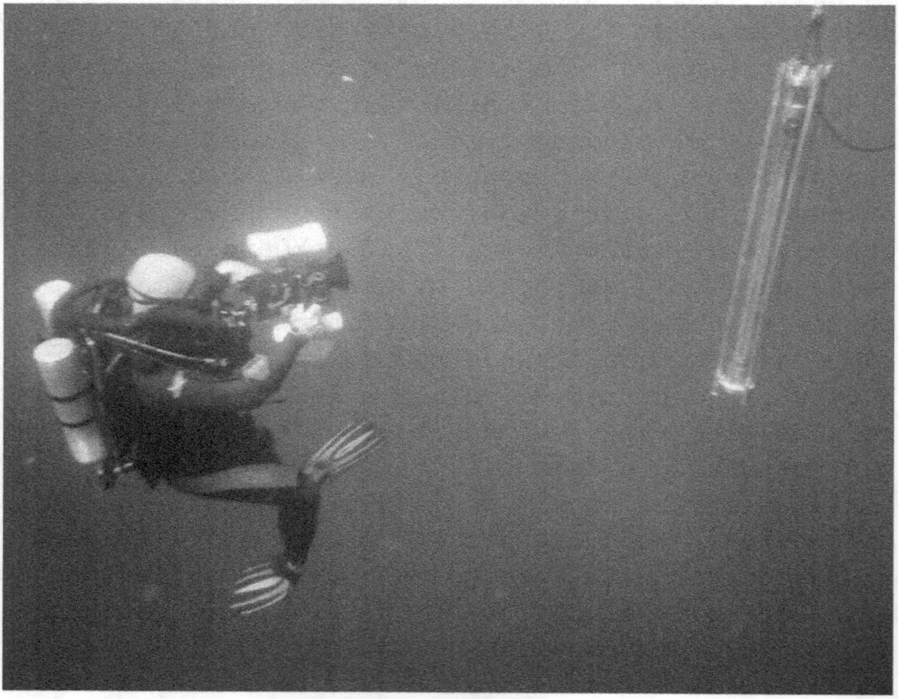

Peter Schalkwijk with *Nereida* Capsule,
Sea of Cortez in Baja California Sur,
México. Photo: Raúl González, 2007

opened up by his research and artwork. Guzik is primarily known for his instruments and sound installations, particularly through his installation *Cordiox* in the Mexican Pavilion of the Venice Biennale in 2013, but my fascination was for this underlyingfieldwork with cetaceans. Guzik told me that his long-term plan was to launch a manned underwater craft and instrument, the *Narcisa*, that would drift unpowered with the circulating currents of theGulf of California, establishing a gentle sound encounter with sea mammals that would unfold through space and time.

We invited the artist and members of his team from the Nature's Expression and Resonance Research Laboratory, of which Guzik is director, to come on an expedition to meet UK cetaceans. Advised by Mark Simmonds, a marine scientist, conservationist and cetaceans expert (whose text appears in this publication), we decided that our expedition would be to the Moray Firth in the North of Scotland, one of the most important places on the British coast for observing dolphins and whales, and in particular to encounter the population of bottlenose dolphins (around 2-300 individuals) that live there.

Ariel Guzik with his collaborators Emilio Galvez and Alejandro Colinas and Arts Catalyst team members arrived on the Black Isle in July 2013 during an unprecedented Scottish heatwave, following his *Cordiox* opening at the Venice Biennale.

The time we spent here, based in the small village of Rosemarkie, included morning walks from our rented house to Chanonry Point to observe dolphins from the shore, and two sea trips by chartered small boat from Cromarty, led by local experts, from which we lowered hydrophones to record the dolphins' clicks and calls as they searched for food or travelled at speed along the Moray Firth. I was surprised at their size, having seen smaller bottlenose dolphins in warmer climates. Moray Firth bottlenose dolphins are large robust creatures, almost the size of small whales, able to thrive in the cold waters of the North Sea and North Atlantic Ocean. The group also met with conservationists and marine scientists, including Professor Paul Thompson and his team at Aberdeen University's Lighthouse Field Station at Cromarty, whose work includes studying migratory patterns and movements of the Moray Firth dolphins. On coming to London at the end of the research trip, Guzik met with Mark Simmonds with whom he discussed the role and vital importance of sound in cetacean society and the devastating impact of sonar and noise pollution on whales and dolphins.

From this expedition, Arts Catalyst and the Edinburgh Art Festival commissioned Guzik to create the second iteration of his cetaceans' project, the *Holoturian*, a larger instrument and capsule. The *Holoturian* capsule is designed to send a living plant and a stringed musical instrument into the deep ocean, as an emissary, an ambassador of the Earth (as humans call this planet) to the Ocean (as cetaceans would know it). Named after a sea echinoderm, *Holoturian* is an iron ship able to dive to great depths. Its external structure is solid, decorated with symbols of an imagined cetacean calligraphy. Inside is a wood cabin housing the plant and instrument, with light, warmth and ventilation to maintain optimal conditions for the plant. The capsule is windowless, designed to be "viewed" primarily by the sonic gaze of whales and dolphins. The stringed instrument emits subtle sounds that seek to evoke echoes of the sea as well as imaginary siren songs and cetacean sounds. The *Holoturian* represents sheltered fragility, its actions under the ocean invisible to human witnesses.

Guzik's research into cetacean communication does not have an investigative intent. Rather he simply seeks to understand, in an intuitive and emotional way, the ways in which cetaceans understand their world and communicate with each other, and to connect with them symbolically as intelligent "others". However, his work raises for me a number of philosophical and to some extent scientific issues, including whether whales and dolphins can be said to have language or culture.

The question of whether any species of whale or dolphin can be said to have language is highly contentious within science, anthropology and linguistics. Academic discussions of whether language exists in non-human animal species tend to compare forms of animal communication with features or properties ascribed to human language. Perhaps it is useful therefore to distinguish "animal communication" from "animal language" in order to discuss whether whales and dolphins communicate in a complex and meaningful way, as well as how they communicate and how we may communicate with them. (Additionally, animal language studies have tended to be conducted with captive animals, which the artist would wish us to avoid.) Recent animal communication research with dolphins has contested the idea that animal communication is less sophisticated than human communication. Denise Herzing has done research with wild dolphins in the Bahamas and shown that they are capable of brilliant and rapid thinking. Other researchers

14

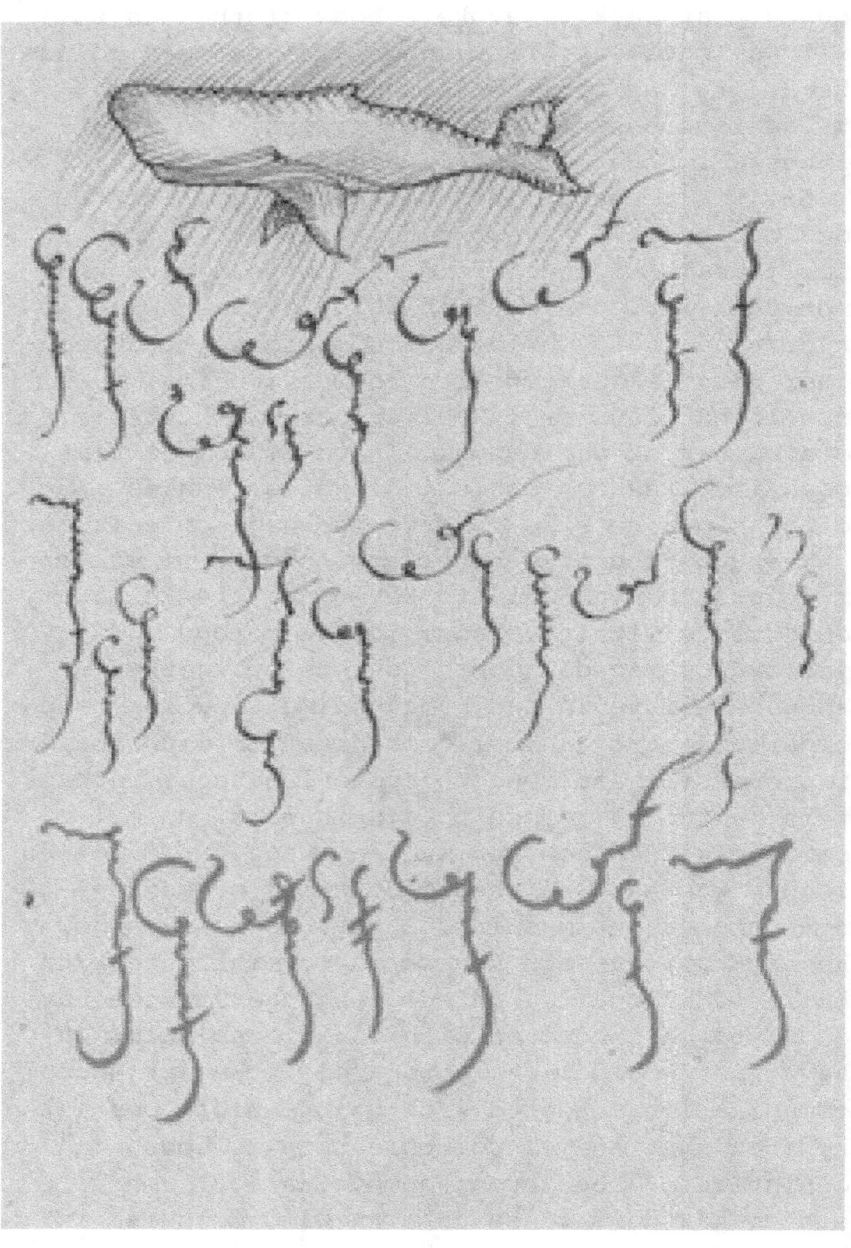

Ariel Guzik, 2014

have discovered that bottlenose dolphin in the wild use whistles to communicate quite complex information, including demographics: their names, ages, and locations. They are capable of vocal learning, referential labelling, syntax comprehension, and joint attention. In their own communication system, these skills are used in individual recognition, group cohesion, and coordination.

An even more hotly debated issue is whether cetaceans — or any nonhuman animal species - can be said to have 'culture'. One difficulty is that the concept of culture, as with language, is entirely human-made. 'Language' and 'culture' are perceived and defined as human properties. It has been assumed, since antiquity, that animals are governed entirely by instinct. Complex animal behaviours — from tool use by chimpanzees to the bowerbird's arty constructions — have been explained as instinctual rather than learned. Scientists and naturalists, such as our advisor Mark Simmonds, who believe that other animals can demonstrate social learning and cultural behaviours, have until recently been a small minority.

A recent book has made a significant contribution to our understanding of cetacean culture. Biologists Hal Whitehead and Luke Rendell, in 'The Cultural Lives of Whales and Dolphins' (2015) respond to this long history of resistance to the notion of animal 'culture' by first carefully defining what they mean by the term. They settle for "Behavior patterns shared by members of a community that rely on socially learned and transmitted information". This may seem, particularly to those who understand culture in terms of art and music, a highly reductive definition of culture and Whitehead and

Rendell themselves arrive at it rather grudgingly, but it should be understood that they are arguing to scientists, and that their arguments and evidence are, in fact, groundbreaking and hold enormous implications for how we regard other animals.

Whitehead and Rendell combine their own decades of research on cetacean behaviour and cognition, and their many direct encounters with marine mammals, with investigation and theory from the biological, physical, and social sciences to describe in great detail the astonishing variety of ways by which whales and dolphins communicate with and learn from each other: from how pods of killer whales in the northeast Pacific benefit from the ecological knowledge of their female elders to how bottlenose dolphins identify themselves individually using signature whistles. Their evidence base for social learning and cultural conformity in cetaceans builds on many other studies (with cetaceans and other animals) in recent years.

Whilst there are numerous definitions of 'culture', there are two main understandings. The first understanding is of culture as the ideas, customs and social behaviours of a particular society, which maps well to the cetacean behaviours described by Whitehead and Rendell in their book and to their definition of culture. The other is of culture as art, music and other manifestations of intellectual achievement, which can be regarded as developments or refinements from the wider culture. The evolutionary biologist John Maynard Smith identified cultural inheritance, the process of learning from others, as the most recent major evolutionary transition in the history of life on earth (and he explicitly recognised cultural inheritance in animals as well as humans). So when Whitehead and Rendell argue that "… when culture takes hold of a species, everything changes. Extraordinary new ideas are developed from old ideas and passed on", this signals the potential for animal culture also to develop and refine. Could animals develop cultural behaviours equivalent to those of art and music? Might they respond to such manifestations of culture from another species — and perhaps more sensitively than we would to theirs? Guzik's cetacean-oriented music hints that we should open our minds to this possibility.

More practically, this new knowledge of whale and dolphin cultural behaviour, Whitehead and Rendell argue "should affect the way we treat cetaceans in practical ways right now, when it comes to effectively conserving them, and as our knowledge grows it may also affect the way we view our responsibilities toward them and our relationships with them." The sceptics, they add, will have to offer more than the dismissive claim, "Oh, whales and dolphins and other animals are only acting as if they have culture, but they don't."

Cultural theorist Donna Haraway also argues against "human exceptionalism" on the basis of some features unique to the former. Instead her book 'When Species Meet' (2008) invites us to understand the human as just another knot in a worldwide web of interspecies dependencies. Whilst primarily Haraway focuses on the human relationship with domestic animals, she usefully suggests a new point of orientation — the term "companion species" - from which to look at animals, and as a different way of theorising relationality and

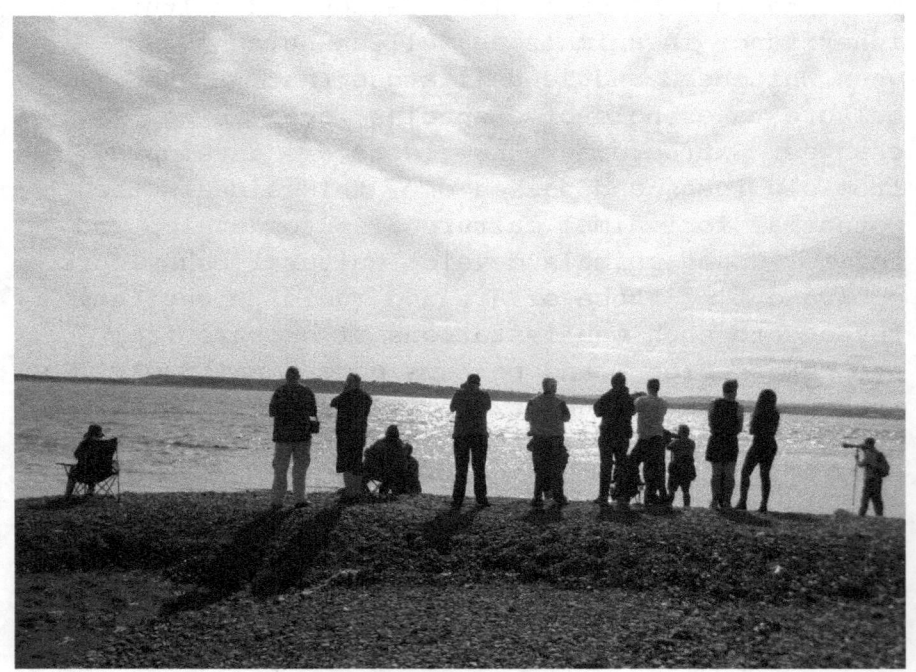

Field trip to Moray Firth with
Ariel Guzik and Nature's Expression
and Resonance Research Laboratory.
Photo: Alejandro Colinas, 2013

co-presence with significant others of all types. Her companion-species approach starts from the premise that "all mortal beings … live in and through the use of one another's bodies". So, whilst acknowledging that pain and suffering is distributed extremely unevenly between human and nonhuman animals, she argues (in her chapter on experimental lab practices), that human beings should learn how to share that suffering by understanding what the animal is going through in order to get this unequal relationship and power structure right.

Guzik's sensitive sound-centred approach also draws our attention to the 'world of sound' within which cetaceans have evolved and existed for millions of years. In his text for this volume, marine scientist and conservationist Mark Simmonds, co-editor of 'Whales and Dolphins: Cognition, Culture, Conservation and Human Perceptions' (2011), explains the complex and social ways in which whales and dolphins use sound to navigate their dark underwater world, as well as to communicate with each other. Simmonds is profoundly concerned about the impact on whales and dolphins of the noise that humans are putting into the oceans, which is altering and disrupting the cetaceans' world.

We also are polluting the cetaceans' world in other ways — plastics, acidification, radioactivity. How can whales and dolphins be protected from human activity?

Whales and dolphins live in the system of interconnected ocean waters that comprise the planet's hydrosphere, which is designated by the United Nations as a 'global commons'. International law identifies four global commons:

the High Seas, the Atmosphere, Antarctica, and Outer Space. Historically, these areas have been guided by the principle of the common heritage of humankind, which holds that these areas should be held in trust for future generations and protected from exploitation by individual nation states or corporations. However, the term 'global commons' has several meanings, which also include a philosophical position suggesting that humankind has both a right and a responsibility to steward the wise use of the Earth for all living species. Increasingly, there are calls for international recognition of cetacean rights, in part an outcome of the growing scientific evidence for self-awareness in bottlenose dolphins, the ability of some whale and dolphin species to communicate individually, their sense of community and the existence of culture in some populations. In 2010, a manifesto was launched entitled 'Declaration of Rights for Cetaceans: Whales and Dolphins', which contends that all whales and dolphins have the right to life, liberty and wellbeing.

Within his installation of the *Holoturian* capsule in the small gothic church Trinity Apse for Edinburgh Art Festival in 2015, Guzik displayed many of his detailed and fantastical drawings that wonderfully depict his evolving ideas for systems of communication with whales and dolphins, including plans and sketches for underwater instruments and submersibles, and images of an underwater cetacean society in reciprocal communication with humans. Guzik's *Holoturian* and drawings have been described as "Verne-esque" and this aesthetic is no accident, springing from the artist's childhood interest in science fiction books and movies. Guzik recounts that he imagined

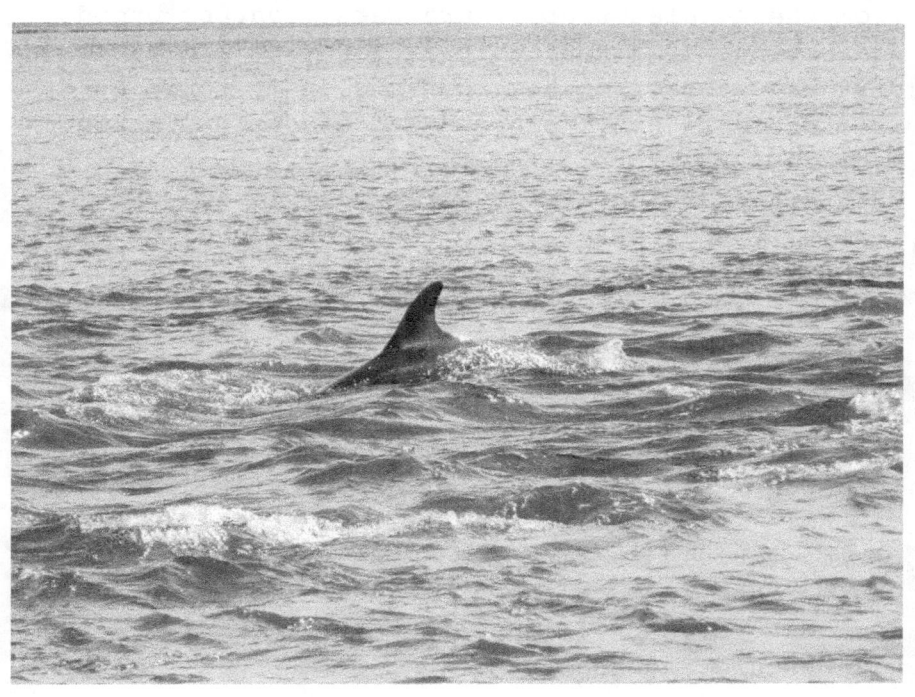

Moray Firth dolphin.
Photo: Alejandro Colinas, 2013

from these tales that future wars might be waged against the machines, corporations and armies of dark predators, but not that the enemy would be as it is today — hazy, blurred and of our own making.

For Guzik, hope lies in encountering new beings on other worlds and discovering new languages. Currently he seeks this in the oceans and the beings that inhabit that other world. At a time when the impact of human activities on our planet is growing exponentially - leading to mass extinctions of plant and animal species, ocean pollution and acidification, and climate change - disillusionment and cynicism are understandable reactions. Artistic visions such as Ariel Guzik's can help us to discover a new enchantment in the world, reviving the profound mysteries of our planet that science seeks to explain yet continues to uncover. Such visions are vital to reconnect us with nature and hope.

Seas of Sound

by Mark Peter Simmonds

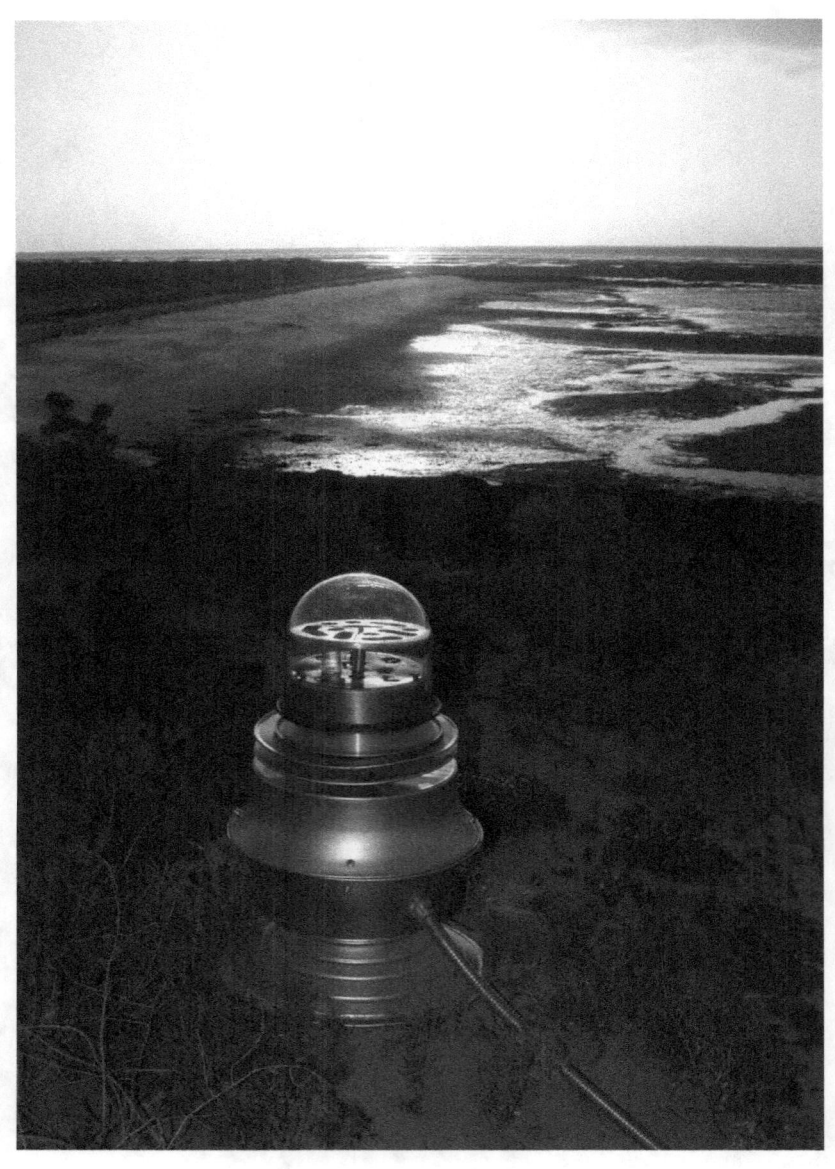

Spectral Harmonic Resonator, Bahía
Magdalena, Baja California Sur, México.
Photo: Raúl González, 2003

Whales, dolphins and porpoises are not like us. Yes, they are mammals. Yes, they breathe air and their mothers suckle their young calves, but their world and their senses are far different from ours. If we want to enter their world, we have to make very elaborate arrangements. We have to take oxygen to breath, insulation to stay warm and, before we have gone too many meters down, even lights so that we can see. Yet we are still missing something fundamental when we do all these things. Even wonderful films of marine life, often artificially illuminated, miss the fact that this is not a world of light and sight like ours but one of sound, where the primary sense of most denizens is hearing! In fact, to put it bluntly, we lack the capacity to listen and comprehend this world in anything like the way that the sophisticated sea creatures do.

25

   The huge blunt head of the sperm whale is essentially a giant oil-filled acoustic organ; arguably the most highly evolved underwater sound production system. Sperm whales make clicks. In fact they make patterns of clicks. The clicks are directed out through the oily mass of tissues in their heads which is, in effect, an 'acoustic lens' that modifies and focuses the sound. The clicks bounce off objects and the returning echoes are heard by the whale and make an acoustic picture in their minds (and they certainly have minds) of the world around them. Many bats, of course, do something similar but the extraordinary acoustic ability of the sperm whale allows it to go into the very deepest seas. Sperm whales can dive to depths of over 1 kilometre and here they feed mainly on deep sea squid. Only they (and a few other similarly equipped whale species) can exploit this deep sea food resource. They find it and catch it mainly using the sounds of their own 'voices' in a place where no appreciable light penetrates. This is marine mammal sonar, equivalent but more sophisticated than the clicks used by submarines to navigate.

Dolphins and smaller toothed whales have similar smaller acoustic lenses and sound producing organs in their heads. Most of them produce two sorts of sounds: high-pitched echolocation clicks to find their way around, find prey, each other and predators; and also lower frequency squeaks, whistles and squeals which are about communicating with each other. All have a remarkably well developed ability to hear. The reason why these animals have hearing as their primary sense is simply physics: sound travels more than four times better in the water than in air and it penetrates the deep and sometimes murky depths far better than light.

Blue whales have incredibly loud and deep voices, below the range of human hearing. Lower frequencies travel further and these massive animals may have the potential ability to signal to each other across hundreds, if not thousands of miles. Their messages at such distances may not be sophisticated but they may be essential. For example they may be announcing their presence to would-be mates that are widely separated. The other big filter-feeding whales have lesser voices but again distant communication is likely to be important for them and something that is incredibly difficult for us to understand and study. (How do you follow whales that are separated over big distances and work out if they are communicating and perhaps coordinating their behaviours?)

It is easy in many instances where such animals are close together to see coordinated activities. One example is coordinated feeding by humpback whales which sometimes make a curtain of bubbles to help corral the fish that they are feeding on, allowing them to scoop them up more efficiently. Then there are dolphins coordinating, not just feeding but also finding mates! And all of this sophisticated activity is held together - coordinated - by sound; the sounds that the animals emit and those that they hear from the surrounding environment.

So if we really want to appreciate the underwater world, we need to 'see' with our ears like them! Our failure to appreciate how important this is — and the difficulties involved in the comprehension of it - is also, in part, responsible for the callous ways in which we have been introducing noise into the oceans. Often this is a by-product For example, boat traffic now provides a constant background drone in the seas and this may mean that whales can no longer hear each other over such great distances this noise pollution masks their calls. It is as if an acoustic 'fog' has descended on the oceans.

Then there are the very loud marine noises that we increasingly make. They don't offend us, indeed typically most of us hardly hear them at all even when we are on the sea because they are not well transmitted from water into air. These include the hammering of mighty pile-drivers in marine construction, the blasts from seismic survey guns — sending pulses through the water into the sea bed to examine the geology there; and the loud noise used by navies to illuminate the oceans as they search for each other. These powerful sounds and others are, of course, affecting sea animals. Evidence is mounting of harassment, stress, wounding and even deaths resulting from noise exposure. The oceans were never silent but we need to still our din, now we know the risks!

I am a big fan of Ariel's work. *Holoturian* reminds me of the big lead fishing weights that my dad used to use. It certainly has that shape of something designed to plumb the depths. But Holothurian also has a very friendly feel to it. Its shape and the sounds that it makes could well draw curious marine animals in for a closer look. In this regard perhaps it constitutes a friendly 'handshake' for those that we cannot converse with directly and it also, importantly for me, it has helpfully invoked more consideration of noise in the oceans and I am grateful to Ariel for this.

Mark Peter Simmonds OBE is Visiting Fellow at the School of Veterinary Sciences of the University of Bristol and the Senior Marine Scientist of the Humane Society International. The views expressed are his own. With others he recently published a review of the emergence of marine noise pollution which can be found here: http://www.thejot.net/?page_id=837&show_article_preview=531

Plates

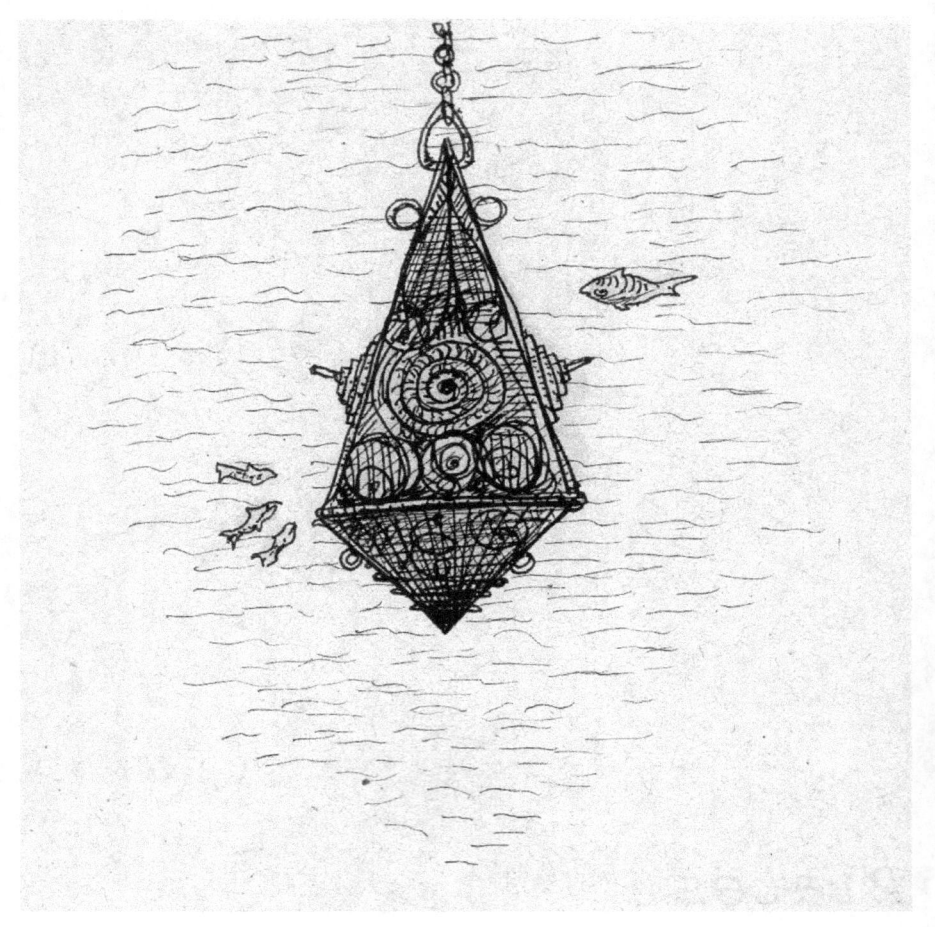

Holoturian, Ariel Guzik, 2015

RIGHT *Holoturian* Exhibition, Trinity Apse. Edinburgh Art Festival, 2015

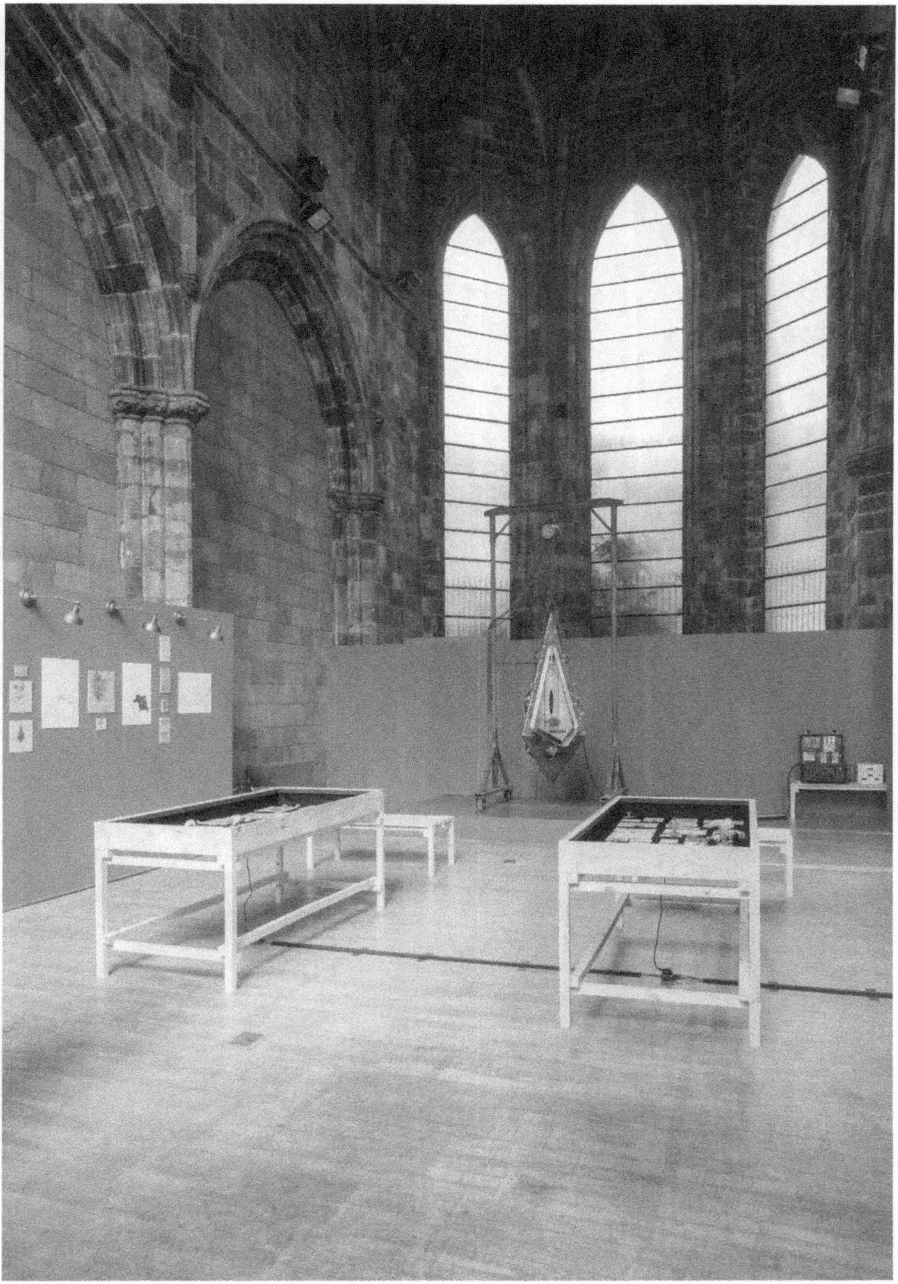

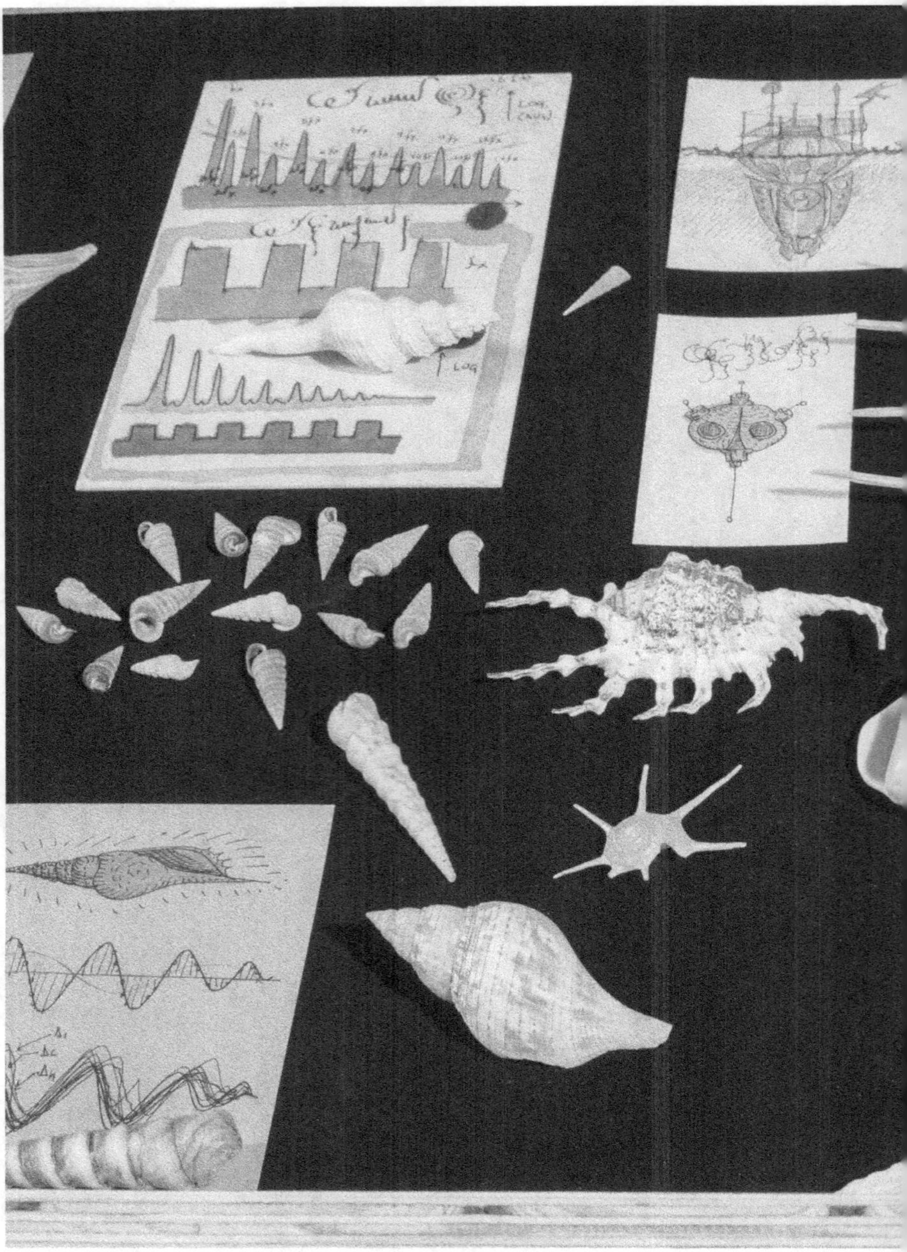

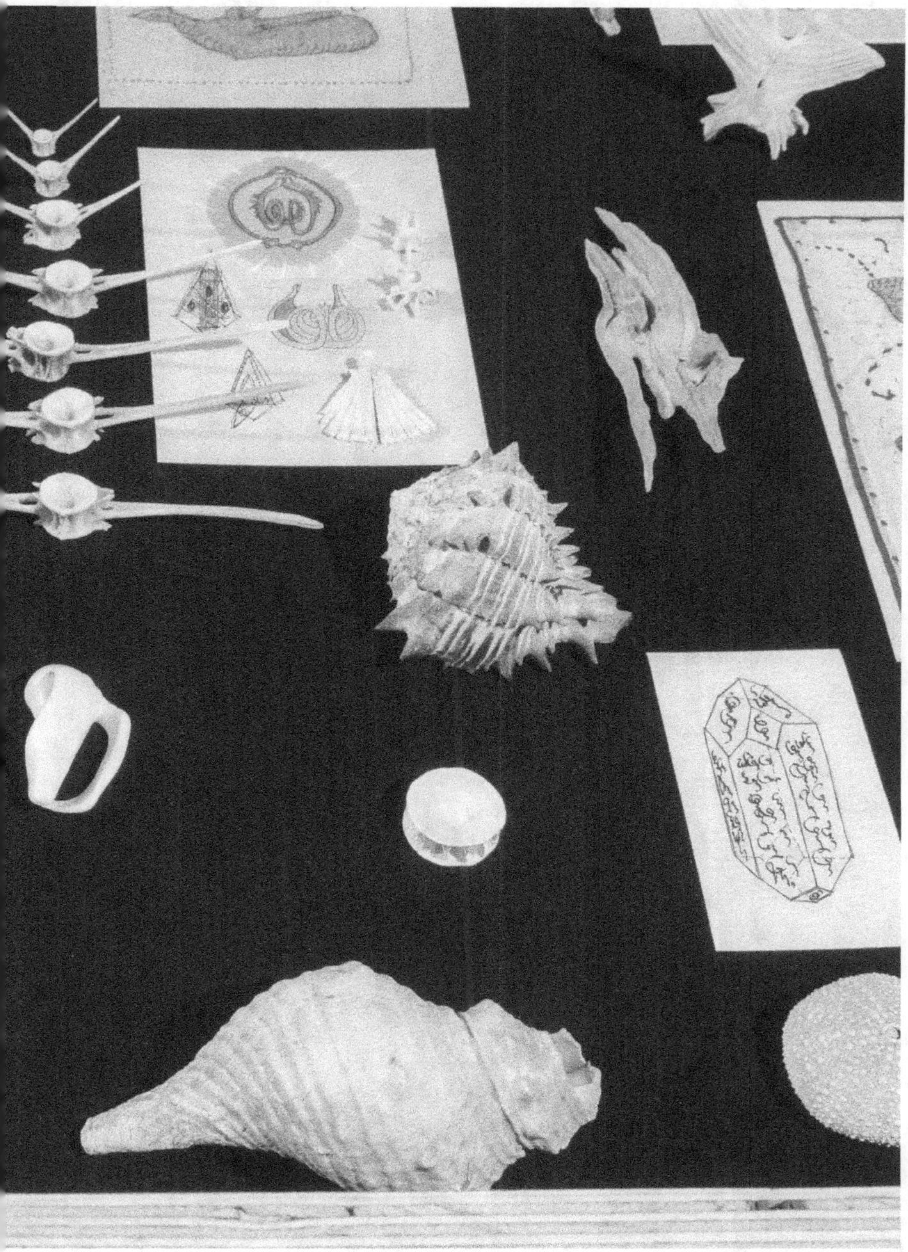

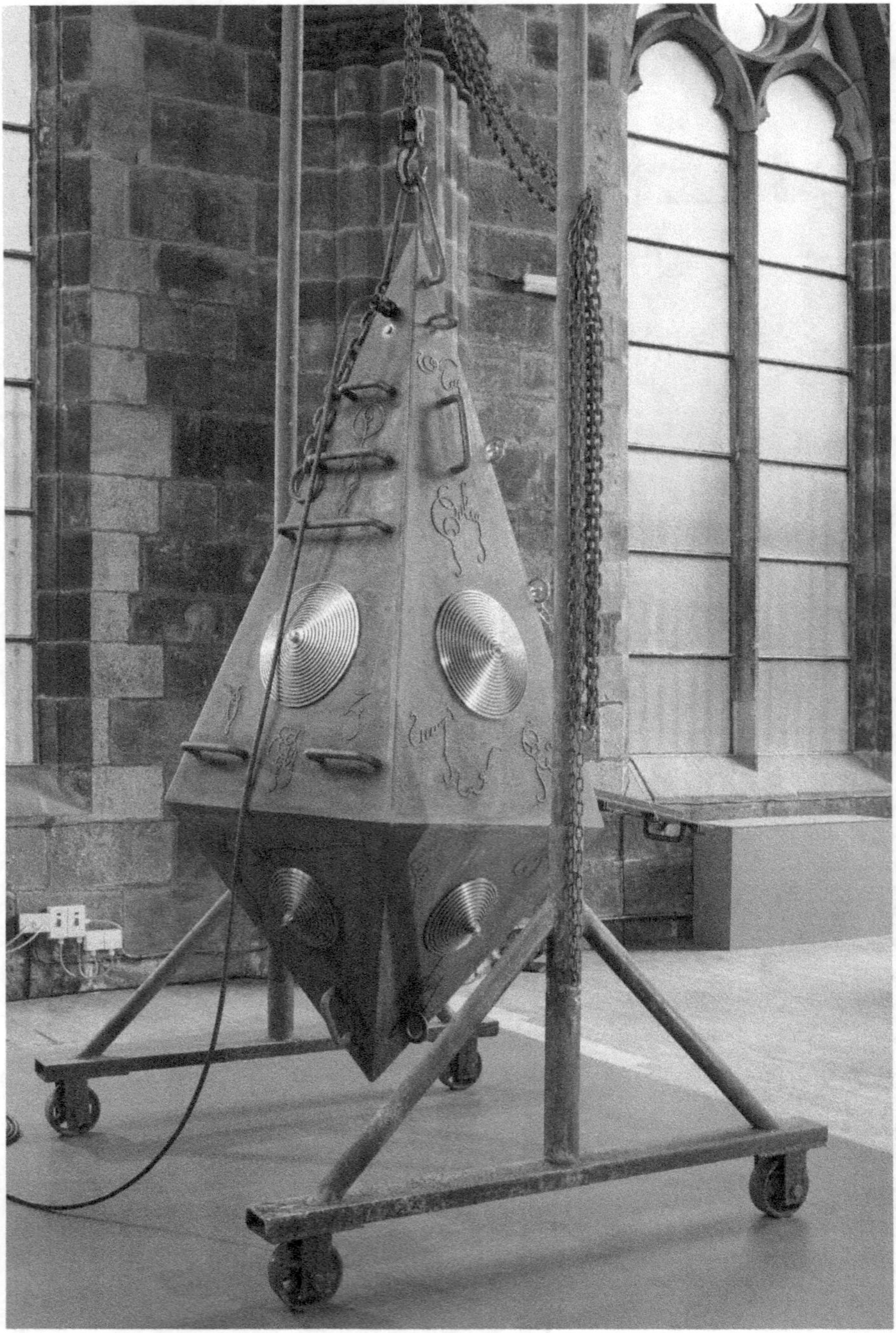

34

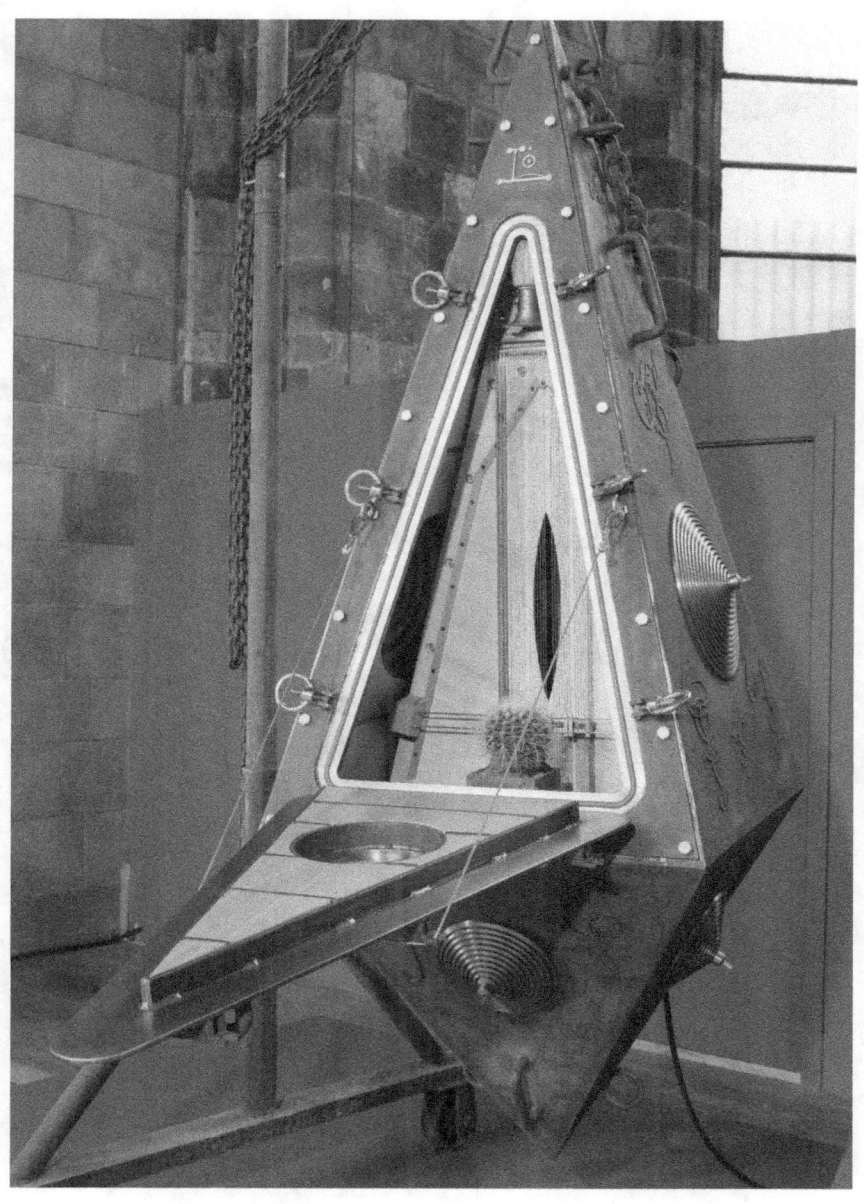

Holoturian Exhibition, Trinity Apse.
Edinburgh Art Festival, 2015

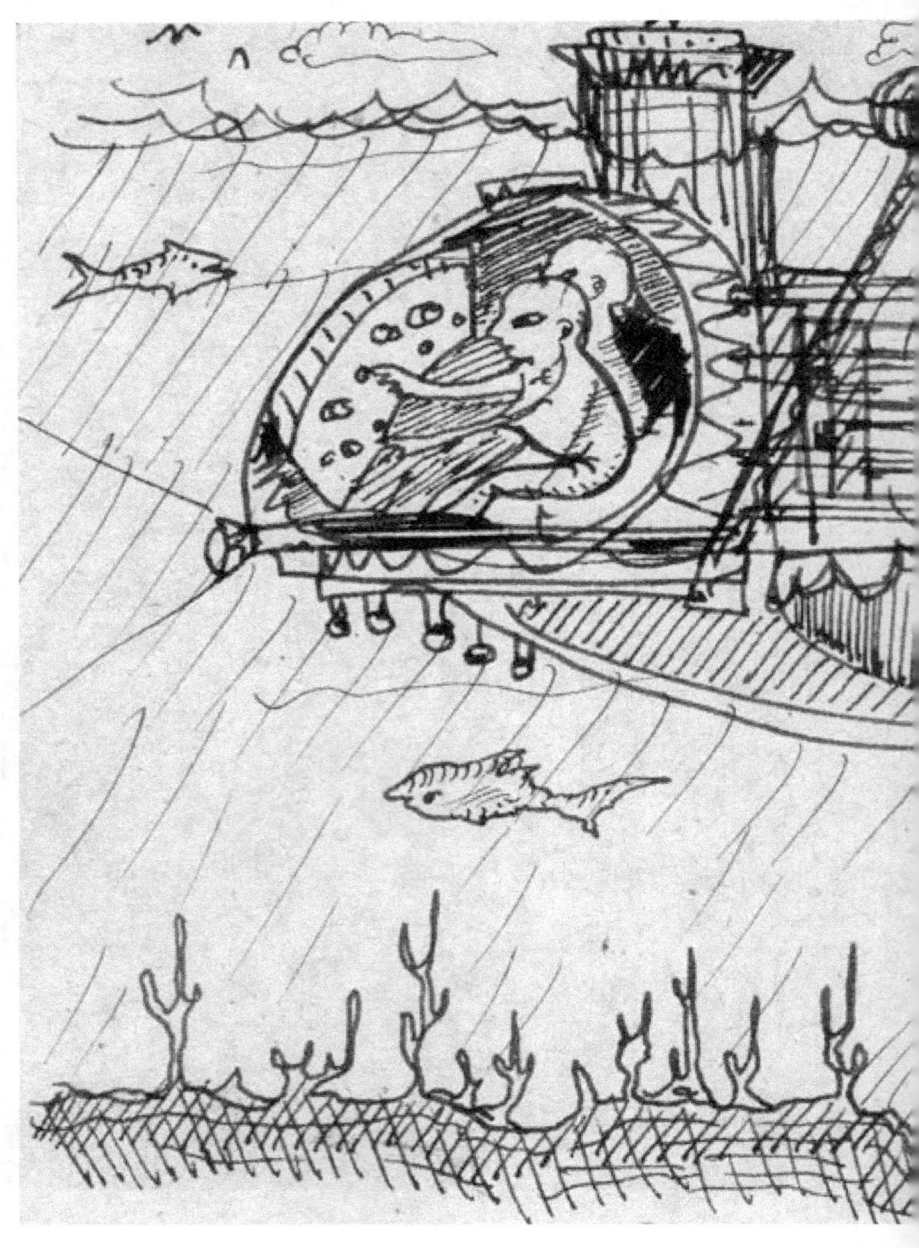

Narcissus Ship, Ariel Guzik, 2010

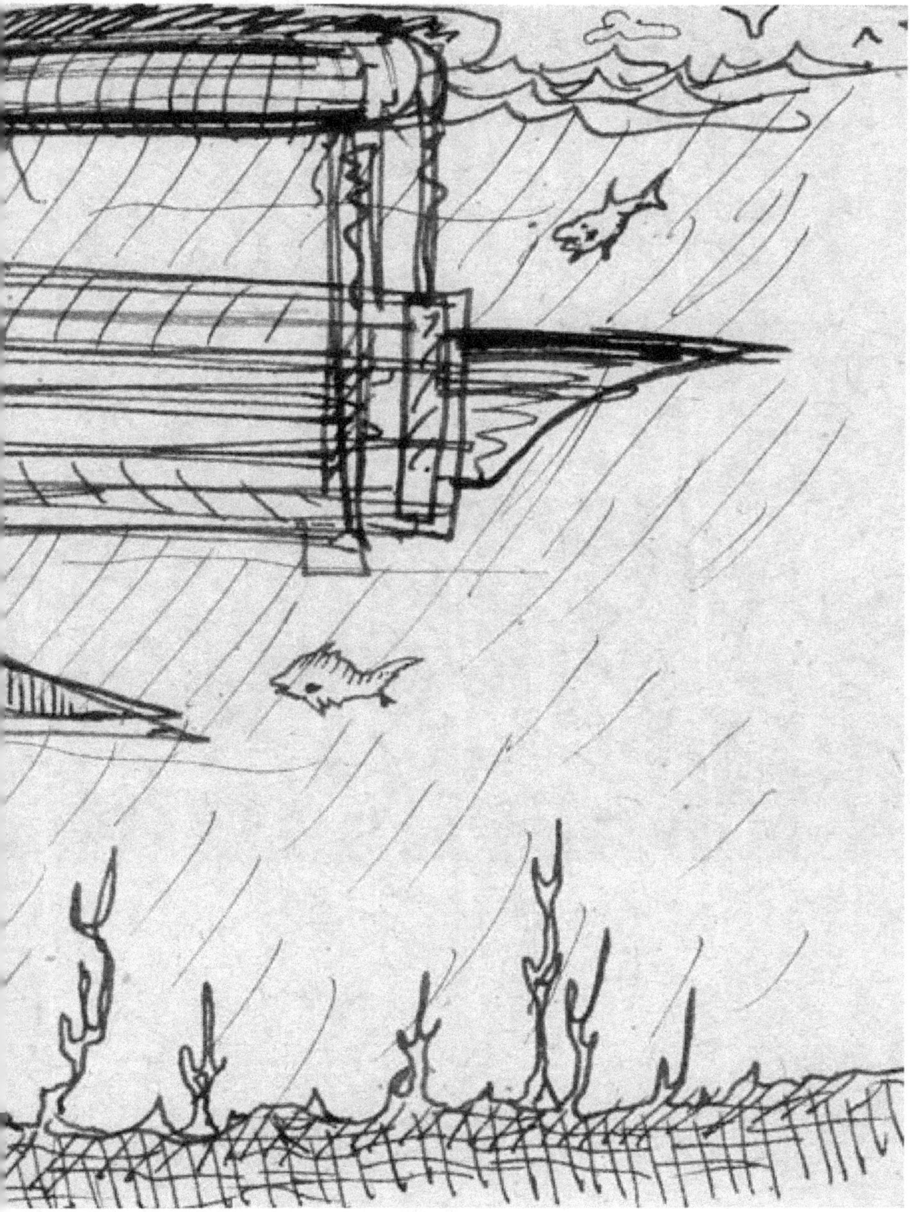

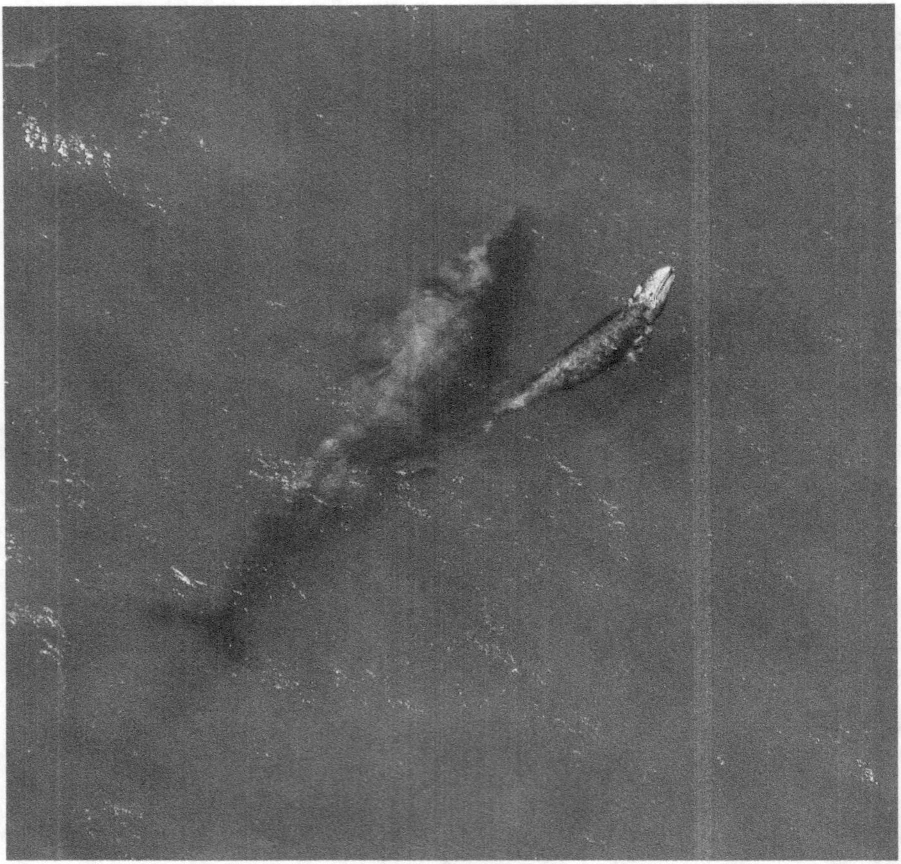

Gray whale and its calf, Magdalena
Bay, Baja California Sur, Mexico.
Photo: Raúl González, 2007

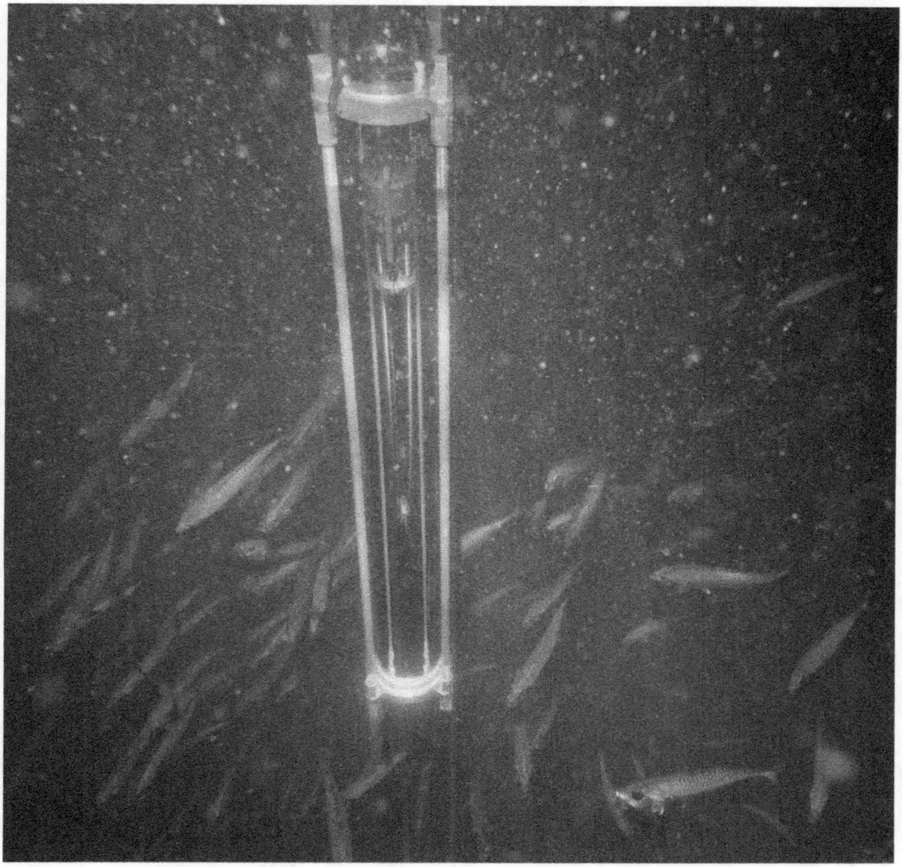

39

Nereida Capsule, Sea of Cortez,
Baja California Sur, Mexico.
Photo: Raúl González, 2012

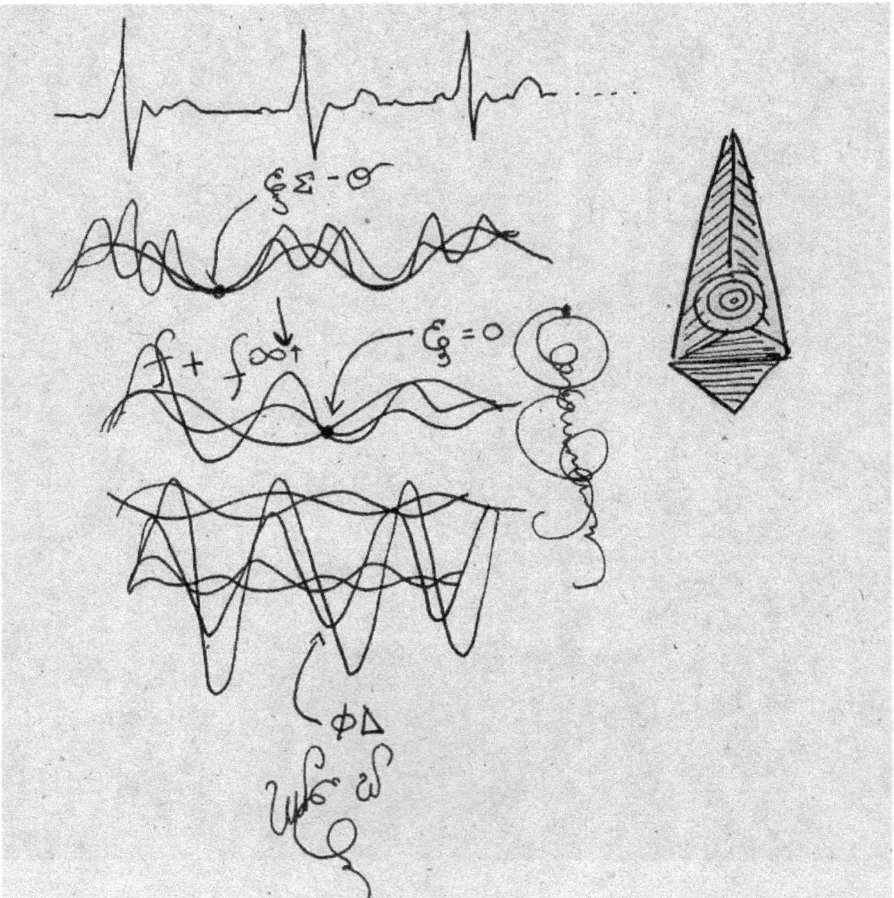

Ariel Guzik, 2015

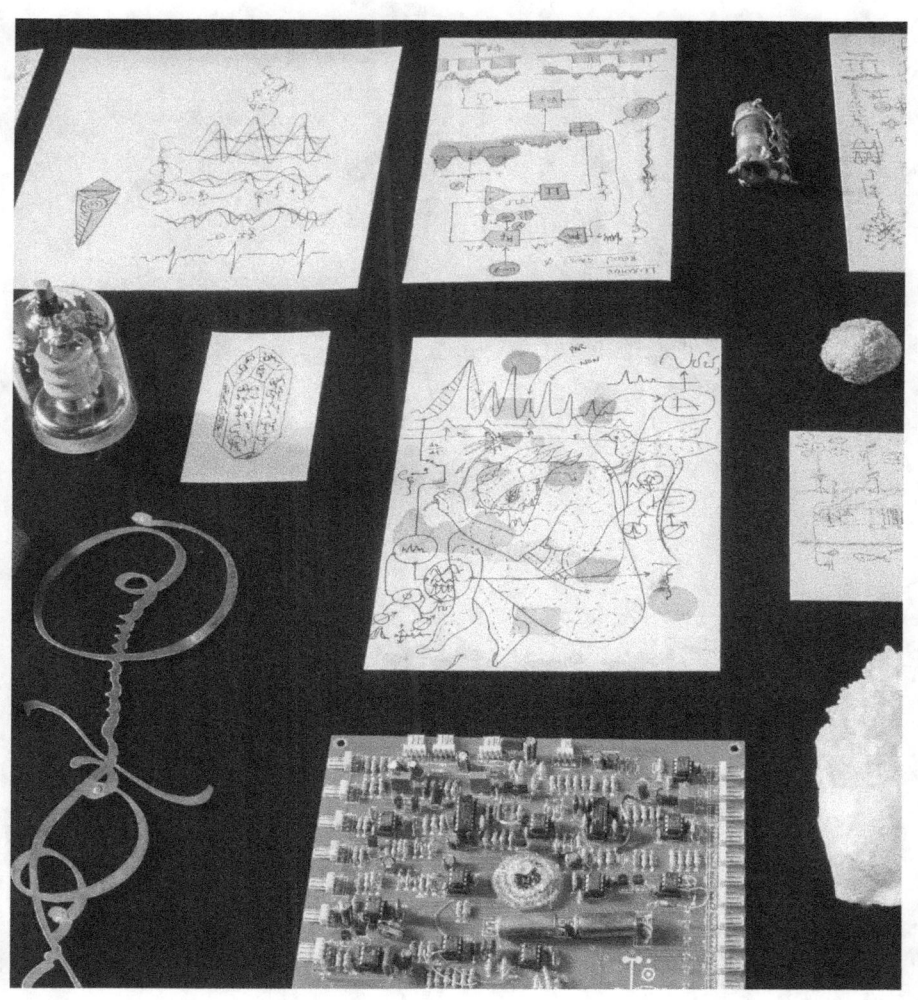

Holoturian Exhibition, Trinity Apse.
Edinburgh Art Festival, 2015

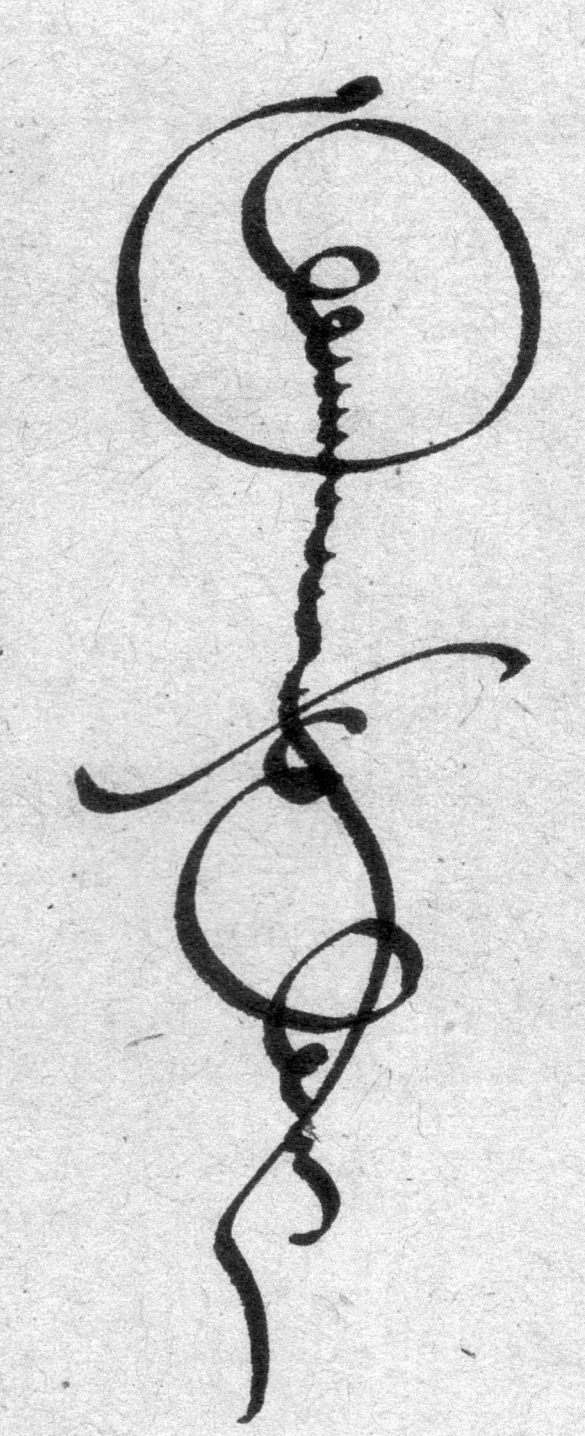

Ariel Guzik's *Holoturian* was commissioned by:

Arts Catalyst and Edinburgh Art Festival 2015

ARTS CATALYST

EDIN BURGH ART FEST IVAL

Ariel Guzik's *Holoturian* research and exhibition was supported by the Wellcome Trust, British Council, Arts Council England, Event Scotland, Museums Galleries Edinburgh and the following Mexican institutions, as part of The Year of Mexico in the UK 15: The Ministry of Foreign Affairs (SRE) through the Mexican Agency of International Cooperation for Development (AMEXCID) The Ministry of Culture (SC), the National Institute of Fine Arts (INBA) and The Anglo Mexican Foundation.

This eBook is supported by:

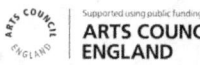 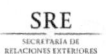

 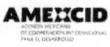 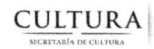

RIGHT *Holoturian*, Ariel Guzik, 2015

www.ingramcontent.com/pod-product-compliance
Lightning Source LLC
Chambersburg PA
CBHW070433180526
45158CB00017B/1173